MUSIC HALL MISCELLANY

Four Riotous Routines

By the same author

IT GIVES ME GREAT PLEASURE
MAKE 'EM LAUGH
THE GOLDEN AGE OF MELODRAMA

Compilations (all Wolfe)

BEST SHOW BIZ JOKES
BEST LEGAL JOKES
BEST TEENAGER JOKES
BEST FOREIGNER JOKES
BEST SERVICE JOKES
BEST BOSS AND WORKER JOKES
MORE BEST RELIGIOUS JOKES
1000 JOKES FOR FUNCTIONS
1000 JOKES FOR KIDS OF ALL AGES

Sketches

THREE MELODRAMAS
THREE MORE MELODRAMAS
INSTANT PLAYS FOR CHILDREN

MUSIC HALL MISCELLANY

by

RICHARD DENNIS

MICHAEL KILGARRIFF

and

MALCOLM SIRCOM

Introduced and edited by

MICHAEL KILGARRIFF

SAMUEL

FRENCH

LONDON

NEW YORK TORONTO SYDNEY HOLLYWOOD

SAMUEL FRENCH LTD, 26 SOUTHAMPTON STREET, STRAND, LONDON WC2E 7JE, or their authorized agents, issue licences to amateurs to give performances of this play on payment of a fee. **The fee must be paid and the licence obtained before a performance is given.**

Licences are issued subject to the understanding that it shall be made clear in all advertising matter that the audience will witness an amateur performance; and that the names of the authors of the plays shall be included on all announcements and on all programmes.

The royalty fee indicated below is subject to contract and subject to variation at the sole discretion of Samuel French Ltd.

Basic fee for each and every performance by amateurs in the British Isles of *The Molecatcher*, *Who Will Man the Lifeboat* and *The Master and the Maid* — Code A

Basic fee for each and every performance by amateurs in the British Isles of *The Tram-Track Tragedy* — Code D

In theatres or halls seating 600 or more the fee will be subject to negotiation.

In territories overseas the fee quoted above may not apply. Application must be made to our local authorized agents, or if there is no such agent, to Samuel French Ltd, London.

ISBN 0 573 00013 1

MADE AND PRINTED IN GREAT BRITAIN BY
LATIMER TREND & COMPANY LTD PLYMOUTH

MADE IN ENGLAND

CONTENTS

PREFACE

Having produced two very successful books of sketches (*Three Melodramas* and *Three More Melodramas*) I thought that in this publication I would try to assemble something a little different in the way of programme fillers for Old Time Music Hall.

Only one of the items in this collection, therefore, is a full-blooded burlesque melodrama: this is *The Tram-Track Tragedy*—in respect of which I would like to acknowledge my debt to Peter and Paddy Ariss of the Tower Theatre, Canonbury, London. *Who Will Man The Lifeboat?* is a musical sketch, an extended treatment of a rousing Sankey tune; *The Master And The Maid* is a novel presentation of the standard melodrama, and *The Molecatcher* is an elaboration of an old rugger song.

Encouraged by the response to my previous two books in this field, I have tried in this volume to be slightly more ambitious; for instance *Who Will Man The Lifeboat?* features a shipwreck, and *The Tram-Track Tragedy* requires the provision of an actual tram! But I am sure that your ingenuity, or failing that the goodwill and imagination of your audiences, will readily supply any deficiencies in the mounting of these masterpieces.

As before, the casts are small and the property lists minimal. But the laughs, I am confident you will find, are enormous.

Michael Kilgarriff

Ealing, November 1976

NOTES TO THE PRODUCER

The Molecatcher

realised by Malcolm Sircom

Running time 10 minutes approximately

This is what is often described as a "strong" routine, by which I am not implying that it is obscene but that it is virtually actor-proof, so that ninety-nine times out of a hundred you can expect it to be a smash. The only danger to its success is that your performers might take it too seriously and start getting all Method and Motivated about it. It is a simple but extremely effective out-front routine which your actors must take on trust and not question too deeply. If anyone asks why one of the characters does this or says that—replace him immediately. You don't want any rationalizing or alienation or heavy cerebrating on this piece—just three strong personalities to follow the text to the letter.

Ever since Malcolm Sircom, who is also a first-rate pianist, writer and composer, introduced *The Molecatcher* into a Music Hall production of mine in 1972 I have featured the routine countless times all over the country, and am always happily confident that it will bring down the first half curtain with a storm of laughter and applause. If this one doesn't send 'em happy to the bars, nothing will.

The three performers should be well contrasted in age and personality, if practicable. A is the eldest but very stupid, perhaps wearing steel-rimmed spectacles and a vacant look. B is the leader; it is his responsibility to control the laughs and ensure that the routine doesn't peak too soon. He can have one or two blacked-out teeth. C is the youngest of the trio, being very much under B's influence. He can have freckles and rosy cheeks. They all have outdoor complexions, but don't overdo the carmine on the cheeks. Beards and moustaches should be varied; ideally A should have a grey "Churdles Ash" beard, B a large droopy moustache, and C clean shaven.

Costumes can either be the traditional smocks with neckerchiefs and straw hats or simply very muddy old raincoats with floppy, battered trilbies. Rough trousers with ropes or straps below the knees and heavy boots should also be worn.

There are few lines to learn in *The Molecatcher* but the gestures should be meticulously rehearsed so that they come precisely together and in time to the musical stresses. The size of the gestures, which should be deliberate and never rushed or snatched, increases with the growing confidence of the performers. Try to remember that there is an actual plot-line in the routine and that it is not just a succession of joey-joeys, so don't let the story get suffocated in the prevailing hysteria. The performers should react to each other's verses as though hearing them for the first time (although A will be a little slow) but watch for the danger of divided attention; the audience's eye must be focused on the right person at the right time, usually by B who must not be allowed to swamp the other two.

Accents are usually "Mummersetshire", but there is no reason why local variations should not be used if desired.

Finally, a word of reassurance: in over four years of presenting this routine all over the country—in Scotland I even put it on with C played by a girl!—I have yet to receive one single word of complaint concerning its "suitability" for O.A.P. matinees, charity shows, family audiences, or for any kind of occasion whatsoever.

Who Will Man The Lifeboat?

devised by Michael Kilgarriff

Running time: six minutes approximately

This unusual but very effective routine had its genesis in a copy of a Breck & Sankey hymn which I came across quite by chance while researching in the British Library. I felt it had possibilities and so copied it out. At home I developed the lyrics into a routine which would feature an actual lifeboat rescue, and adapted the music to fit the conception. It was over two years before I had the chance to see it on stage, but the wait was worth it because the routine, beautifully played by a marvellous cast, was an outstanding success, being greeted with loud and prolonged applause. Not to mention the laughs which were more frequent than we had anticipated, and that is always a pleasant surprise.

The staging is not difficult and there is not a great deal to learn; there are two main problems—the similarity of the verse to the chorus, musically speaking, which makes it confusing for the players, and the technical problems of the boat-truck.

Of the suggested settings, only the groundrow is necessary—and even that can be dispensed with if the steamship is carried across by someone dressed from head to foot in black. The steamer will need to sink behind a black cloth. The mariner in distress can in this instance, therefore, pop his face through the upstage runners at the appropriate moments; if the runners are pinned together to about five feet above the stage he can wave his arms about while standing on a chair, and can be lifted through quite easily.

The elaborations of setting—bathing-tent, breakwater, pier cut-out, lobster-pots, etc., are only suggested if there is to be a lengthy seaside scena of which this routine is forming just a part.

Lighting is important; the areas to be separated are DR where the three ladies stand, LC where the lifeboat first appears; the bathing-tent entrance (or UR). A special will also be needed for the coat of arms, if you can run to it. A follow spot should pick up the mariner whenever he appears, also Britannia. Apart from the areas listed the lighting should be low—don't forget there is a storm raging—and the lightning kept going, at decreasing intervals, until the rescue.

It is because the lighting is moody throughout that I think it better to follow this routine with a jolly chorus song to give you a chance to bring the lights up for a couple of minutes before the interval.

The chairman's preamble is only necessary if this routine comes out of the blue; if you already have a seaside scena in progress it is better to have a song interrupted by the storm and go directly into the appearance of the steamer.

The mariner should be short or light or both as he has to be lifted and shaken; he alone of the cast need not be a good singer—his solo lines can be spoken provided the rhythm is not lost. His appearances above the waves should be mimed as in slow motion; his mouth clearly indicates a desperate "HELP!" as he points pathetically to himself and sinks out of sight. These brief appearances raise enormous laughs and so should be placed and timed strictly as given in the text or the routine will come adrift. He should be panicky, pathetic, but not effeminate. To make him "poofy" would undoubtedly get some easy laughs, but, in my opinion, unworthy ones. He should be dressed in rags and barefoot, which will give him something slightly over one minute to change if you continue with "Beside The Seaside". The bathing-costume can be underdressed, of course.

The alto's costume for Britannia will be a simple full-length backless "alb" which she can put on back to front and fasten at the wrists and back of the neck with velcro. Her shield should be permanently fixed to the DS side of the boat; she can steady herself by holding on to this. The spear likewise can be wired in place.

The ladies should dress in simple but colourful summer day dresses of the period with matching hats and R.N.L.I. sashes across their bosoms. The props—tambourine, collecting-box and bass-drum—if possible should also match their user's colour scheme, and while I realize this is possibly a counsel of perfection I hope it will demonstrate one of the little ways in which a routine like this or of any kind can be given just those extra touches which help to make it something special.

If the stage is being used a great deal immediately prior to the boat-truck's appearance, the problem arises of how to get the trick line across. This can be solved by the chairman simply crossing the stage with his umbrella either to the pianist or to make an exit and taking one end with him. If it is the free end there is no problem, if the other, there is plenty of time for it to be hooked up to the truck.

The truck should be about eight feet long but need not be more than eighteen inches wide; the boat cut-out (which should include a bit of sea) will need to be about three feet in height. One-directional castors, six in all, should be used to stop it gliding about; on a flat stage one person will be quite able to pull the truck on, and a considerable speed can be attained for Britannia's exit.

The design of the boat should represent the lifecraft on the traditional R.N.L.I. collecting-box and, as I have already said, be resting in its own piece of ocean.

The singing must be as good as you can get, with the harmonies accurate and secure. There are a surprising number of laughs in this routine, and the effect is greatly enhanced if musically it is of a high standard. Don't let your mariner go too far: no prop fish or Marx Brothers burlesquing. His fear of drowning should be real as well as comic; similarly your alto as Britannia should really act the pride and nobility of the greatest Empire the world has ever known; again, you don't want any cheap mugging as the boat bears her off at ever-increasing speed. Just a hint of panic in the eyes and a convulsive grip on the shield, maybe, but the final triumphant "slaves" should not waver.

The laughs build slowly in this one; let your audience discover the comedy for themselves. The chuckles will build to shrieks as the mariner appears, and then Britannia's entrance will raise positive screams—her exit, if properly timed, bringing a furore of laughter and applause.

Don't bring up the lights too soon after her exit; an audience loves to show its appreciation. I don't think it is a good idea to bring the cast on for a call; continue your programme in one of the three ways I have indicated at the end of the text. If necessary, your artists can be acknowledged in the programme.

The full piano and vocal score is given on page 60.

The Tram-Track Tragedy

by Johnny Dennis and Michael Kilgarriff

Running time: 25 minutes approximately

Despite the ludicrous plot and the joey-joey gags, the playing of all the characters in this sketch should be informed by a certain degree of truth and integrity. Don't let your company guy their roles—the piece is already a burlesque so to push the drollery any further will just result in half an hour of tedious silliness. Nellie can be genuinely touching in her naïvety, and Claud, in his credulous, bumbling, flat-footed way, can also seem quite affecting. Encourage your cast to aim for substance as well as comedy and you will be offering a grateful audience rather more than they (or you) had bargained for. And a surprise bonus is always welcome.

There should be plenty of punch and pace, without letting the plot become obscured. The audience will really want to know the outcome (provided your actors have generated sufficient interest in the characters) so don't let important points get lost. The first mention of the villain's name (by Nellie) should be thrown out carefully and clearly—it is, after all, a very unusual one. Belle's "Quick! Quick—it's getting closer!" immediately prior to the appearance of the second, larger tram, is also vital, both to the plot and to the success of the gag. Lemuel's amazing revelations and costume and character changes should be done swiftly but deliberately, so that the audience is able to keep up with the plot and not become confused. Similarly, let the whiffen-poof be seen and savoured by the audience before it disappears (this business can be cut if it is not workable on your stage).

There is one stylistic point I have always insisted on in my own productions, and it is one which I have constantly reiterated in my various publications on the subject: your actors, while speaking, should always (or nearly always) **look out front**. The trick is to look out front while **speaking** and then to face the next speaker while **listening**. For example:

Claud (*looking into the basket*) But what is this?
Nellie (*crossing* DLC. *Looking out front*) Er . . . this is my child, Claud. (*With a nervous smile*) *Our* son . . .
Claud (*still looking at the basket in dismay*) Oh . . . (*He looks at Nellie open-mouthed, then out front. In hurt, recriminatory tones*) I've been away three years, Nellie . . . ?
Nellie (*after a fraction's pause for thought, with an angelic smile out front*) But you wrote such *lovely* letters, Claud . . .

This exchange was received with screams of laughter—of course, Barrie Gosney's hurt, perplexed expression and Jacqueline Clarke's razor-edge timing (she gave the minutest pause before "lovely") had a lot to do with it—and gives you some idea of what I mean by "out-front playing". It is not easy to achieve, and you may meet some initial resistance from your cast, but it is an essential technicality of melodrama playing and should be insisted upon.

Keep it all crackling along; the rehearsal running-time of the piece should not be longer than eighteen minutes. Keep the entrances crisp; have your actors spring on, facing front, to deliver their first lines on the instant. Get them off sharply also, perhaps being overlapped by the next line. Have all cues picked up slickly, and tell your actors firmly not to be afraid to go back on a line if, in performance, a laugh takes them unawares. Ploughing on regardless through laughs is the besetting sin of the amateur, and not a few professionals, I regret to say.

Belle's line about the widow of the poor bookmaker should be altered to suit the occasion, i.e. if you are performing for the Barclays Bank A.D.S. she might say "only the widow of a poor bank director, 'tis true." Similarly, Belle's line "Was that the man from the Pru?" (which *must* be delivered out front) can be altered to suit.

Lemuel should be played by your most protean actor. I was lucky enough to have in the part David Tate, a well-known West End musical comedy and revue artiste, who has the knack of suggesting remarkably complex characterisations in a very economical manner. His gypsy sounded like Bela Lugosi and seemed thick-lipped and slack-jawed; his messenger was all bright-eyed, bushy tailed and epicene; his conductor was an avuncular Cockney; and his Hawkshaw was as stolid as the Rock of Gibraltar, all heavy nasal tones and downward inflections. Just his first word as the detective—"Hawkshaw!"—was received with a roar of mirth.

The villain is usually the role which suffers most from inexperienced playing; keep Sir Putrid fast and mean rather than ponderous and histrionic. Johnny Dennis, an old hand in melodrama villains, scuttled about the stage like a malevolent beetle; he kept the gestures to a minimum and relied on his eyes, and especially his eyebrows, for subtlety of expression.

Nellie can also suffer from being too slow. Keep her as bright and as perky as the situation allows; much the same can be said of Belle, who has a great deal of important plot to impart and so must have impeccable delivery. The very attractive Adrienne Frank sasshayed sensually around the stage in this role, belting out her informatory lines and keeping the show moving along where it was needed.

Claud blunders about short-sightedly and perhaps even a touch pathetically; if he has a rather querulous tenor speaking-voice it will contrast well with the other two men in the cast, both of whom will speak in deepish tones.

Movements should be clean-cut and largely formalized—especially the ladies, who should move from attitude to attitude in an almost balletic manner. Claud might be rather untidy in his movements, since he is played by a not very "good" actor. Barrie Gosney—another superb revue man—managed to convey a quite remarkable duality in his performance, in that he was obviously a "bad actor" doing his best to be heroic, while simultaneously contriving to be genuinely believable and quite affecting.

In this book I have set out the production moves, business and gags exactly as we performed them, i.e. with the piano on stage DR and the chairman DL. We had no proscenium arch so I put up two screens on either side, giving space about the size of a W.C. cubicle for wings. Lemuel and Sir Putrid were smuggled up during the preceding interval, while the other members of the cast, as indicated in my text, entered from out front, down the centre aisle of the auditorium and up steps C on to the stage. If you have proper wings, then your chairman may prefer to sit DR and if your piano is in the pit then it is no difficult matter to alter my stage directions to suit.

I have given details concerning the working of the two trams on page 45, also instructions for the whiffenpoof. The piano/vocal score from the appearance of the first tram until the end of the sketch is given on page 69.

If your show in in three parts, this sketch could occupy the whole of Part Two—by the time the piano has played a couple of entr'acte choruses, your chairman has given the Loyal Toast, congratulated any birthday or wedding anniversary celebrants in the audience and told a couple of gags,* ten minutes will have gone by before the sketch even starts! If, however, your show is in two parts it would be best to open the second half with this piece; after it either the chairman can offer a chorus song or one of the two ladies in the sketch, still in costume and in character, can oblige with a suitable popular (not comic) song.

* See my own *It Gives Me Great Pleasure* (Samuel French), the handbook for Music Hall Chairmen.

The Master And The Maid

by Michael Kilgarriff

Running time: approximately 6 minutes

This sketch is short, simple and extremely effective; but it requires disciplined rehearsal and experienced playing. Costumes and make-up should suggest the primitive movie-making of the turn of the century, while all your cast's movements should be jerky, angular and very stagey. Remember that the camera did not move in those days (there was no tracking or panning and even close-ups were virtually unknown) so film acting was not much different from poor theatre acting—very crude and all "out front". Because sound had not been developed the pantomiming was broad, and speech always appeared very curious, with eyebrows waggling wildly and lips and teeth working nineteen to the dozen. (There are several opportunities for speech in this sketch where this should be borne in mind.)

Much of the comedy is derived from the reversing of the original plot, and the strange results which this gives rise to. For instance, the husband appearing to lay his chin on the lover's fist, the lover seeming to offer his ear to the husband; the careful donning of his topper by the husband, whereupon he immediately removes it. Then there are the various occasions where people show surprise *before* something untoward occurs, after which they appear quite unconcerned.

The third run (i.e. the second forward run) of the sketch should be as fast as your actors can manage it without falling over themselves; the slow-motion and full-stop during the fight sequence can be omitted, but if you leave it in it should be accompanied by a suitable slowing down of the ad lib piano accompaniment. There should be no accompaniment during the reversing run.

The whirring sound should come from the rear of the auditorium (a bicycle wheel works admirably) and not through a P.A. system, which only sounds distractingly anachronistic.

If you cut out the slow-motion sequence you can also cut out the French projectionist's lines entirely, since his first "appearance" is only to set him up for the later contretemps. If your Frenchman is visible, dress him in evening clothes, plus an Imperial beard and slim moustaches.

The flicker-lime is discussed on page 46 in connection with *The Tram-Track Tragedy*; for this sketch a strobe light is the ideal since it assists very considerably with the jerky movement effect that your cast will be working so hard to achieve.

The handkerchief leaping from the floor. This is worked by having a length of carpet twine attached to one corner of the handkerchief which passes up the husband's right sleeve and down to his right waistcoat pocket where it is secured by being tied to a small toggle of wood or ball or anything suitably hard and small. As the husband bends down to place the handkerchief on the floor with his right hand he simply reaches into the waistcoat pocket with his L hand, takes hold of the toggle and then, with this concealed in his hand, he raises his hand in mock despair and the hanky will leap from the floor into his right hand. Obviously this will need careful adjusting depending on the height of your husband—give him some twine and ask him to practise at home.

The re-appearance of the duster in the maid's hand can be achieved most simply by the maid holding out her hand quite close to the L exit so that someone off stage can place the duster-handle in her hand; for this method her positioning is quite critical and depends on the length of the duster-handle since you will want as much of the head to show as possible. However, if you have black drapes as a background (which is quite acceptable) the duster can be placed in her hand by an arm covered in black; this will not be seen (especially in the flicker) and will allow the maid to "retrieve" the duster standing well on stage. Also, the duster can describe a convincing arc from the wings before landing in her hand.

The vital element in this sketch is, of course, precision of movement; I have seen it performed many times and can testify to the pleasure of the spectators lying not only in the inherent humour of the sketch but in the sheer enjoyment of watching a slick, polished and original routine. The audience is always one pace behind so do not try to make the reverse run totally exact—this would be well-nigh impossible to achieve and would probably look more peculiar than comic. It is sufficient to *suggest* a reversal, with the cast walking backwards, reacting before events, etc., etc.

There is considerable strength in this sketch; the fascination of the unexpected will amply repay your rehearsal time.

THE MOLECATCHER

This version was first presented by Sir Arthur Dunster's celebrated Old Time Music Hall in Whitbread's Cellars, Chiswell Street, EC1, for the City of London Festival, in July 1972. The performers were as follows:

Chairman	Michael Kilgarriff
A	Kim Grant
B	Norman Warwick
C	Maurice Walsh

The routine was directed by Malcolm Sircom

Notes for the first verse and chorus are given on page 58. The verses can be taken quite steadily—as there is no accompaniment each soloist can pick his own tempo. The choruses should be sung slightly quicker with a brief pause on each "day".

THE MOLECATCHER

Chairman At this point in the programme we have the dubious privilege of greeting three of those dirty old—grand old yeomen of England who have made this country what it is today. These three gentlemen are in considerable demand for various entertainments in their village and the surrounding area where their performances have so often been tried, tested and found wanting. But this is their very first visit to the great Metrollops of . . . (*local*), and they are very nervous indeed, so I want you to give them a nice, warm, friendly welcome as they bring us now a fine old English folk tale entitled "The Molecatcher". So let's have a big clap for the Three Mangelwurzels!

Enter A, B and C to the strains of "To Be A Farmer's Boy". A leads on from whichever side is the more convenient, hanging on to his smock-tail is B with C hanging on to B's smock-tail. A, who is the eldest and the most stupid, stands down RC *facing upstage; B, who is the leader and the most ebullient, stands down* C *facing the audience; C is the youngest and also faces the audience. He stands down* LC. *They stand for a moment or two looking round like scared rabbits when B notices that A is facing the wrong way. He tries to attract A's attention without success; he looks worriedly at* C, *who looks helpless, and at the Chairman, who motions them to get on with it. Eventually B pulls A round—quite slowly and gently—and when A sees the audience his face registers horror. B and C cough to cover their embarrassment and A does the same, but C goes a little too far by placing one index finger against his nose and taking a deep breath. Obviously he is about to blow his nose but B stops him in time*

This is the cue for the pianist to play the key-note; the performers look at him blankly, or do not hear, whereupon the pianist then sings the note softly in a manner which suggests the bleat of a sheep. The three men pick up the note and within seconds are running through the entire farmyard population—cows, cockerels, etc. Eventually, they settle down and A starts, very hesitantly. The piano is tacet until the lead off

A In Ambleside (*or local*) village, at the sign of the plough,
There lived a molecatcher, and I'll tell you now:
B Singin . . .
Omnes Fol-de-rum-day,
Fol-de-rum-day,
Fol-de-rum, diddle-um-diddle-um-day.

The last line of the chorus should be sung quite quickly with the three men still very uncertain of their audience. After quite a pause, during which they look at each other for mutual support, B reluctantly continues:

B He went a-mole-catchin', from mornin' till night,
And a young fella come for to . . . play with his wife!
singin . . .
Omnes Fol-de-rum-day, etc.

The word "play" in the verse should be accompanied by a slight waggling of the fingers of the right hand, with the wrist bent forward. This gesture is also used by all three during the succeeding chorus; the movement should be in accord with the musical phrasing, and the left hand should be still. This gesture should be quite small; the audience's reaction will be taken up by B who rapidly loses his nervousness and starts enjoying himself

C Now the molecatcher, jealous of this very same thing,

He hid in the shi—wash-house . . .

There is usually a very big laugh on this; B looks shocked, and exchanges worried glances with A and the audience

. . . to see 'em come in.
B Singin . . .
Omnes Fol-de-rum-day, etc. (*They gesture as before, but this time also bring the hand up slightly. If the audience reaction warrants it, B can extract further laughs by doing the gesture solo after the chorus is finished*)
A Now as the young lad climbed over the style,
It caused the molecatcher so crafty to smile—he he!

B Singin . . .

Omnes Fol-de-rum-day, etc. (*This time a clenched fist is brought up slightly*)

B The lad knocked at the door, and this he did say:
"Oh, where is your husband, good woman, I pray?"
Singin . . .

Omnes Fol-de-rum-day, etc. (*The clenched fist is brought up very sharply so that the fore-arm is horizontal. By this time all three have quite lost their fear of the audience*)

C "He's gone a-mole-catchin', you need have no fear";
But little they thought the molecatcher was near!

B Singin . . .

Omnes Fol-de-rum-day, etc. (*This time the fist rises to the shoulder, with the left hand on the fore-arm. Keep the gestures together and in time with the music*)

A She went off upstairs, he followed her sign;
And the crafty molecatcher crept up her—crept close up behind!

This is a "genuine" slip of the tongue, which vexes A mightily and produces consternation in B and C

B Singin . . .

Omnes Fol-de-rum-day, etc. (*This chorus utilizes all the gestures employed so far, each different gesture coming on successive stresses*)

B Now as the young lad was in the midst of his frolics,
The molecatcher caught him quite hard by the bo——

But before he can get the appalling word out the other two have clapped their hands over B's mouth. He is enraged and quite a struggle ensues, with A and C being dragged all round the stage. Eventually B breaks free and sings the chorus on his own, very fast and aggressively. He is livid at having his big moment spoilt, but soon recovers his good humour

C Now . . . (*This merely to attract attention*)
The trap it bit tight, (*link fingers with hands open and palms facing the floor*)
And he laughed at the sight, (*bring palms together sharply*)
Saying, "Here's the best mole I ever caught in my life!" (*Twist wrists so that the back of the right hand is facing the audience,*

then waggle the right index finger. This last line should also be sung diminuendo and with the knees bending progressively lower)

B Singin . . .

Omnes Fol-de-rum-day, (*link fingers with hands open and palms facing the floor*)
Fol-de-rum-day, (*bring palms together sharply*)
Fol-de-rum-diddle-um-diddle-um-day! (*Twist wrists so that the back of the right hand is facing the audience, then waggle the right index finger. As on the previous verse this last line should be sung diminuendo and with the knees bending progressively lower*)

A I'll make you pay well, for ploughing my ground,
The fee it will cost you no less than ten pound!

B Singin . . .

Omnes Fol-de-rum-day, (*Gesturing with clenched fists*)
Fol-de-rum-day, (*Fist up to shoulder with left hand on fore-arm*)
Fol-de-rum (*Hands linked*)
Diddle-um (*Palms brought together*)
Diddle-um-day. (*Waggle little finger, sink at knees, diminuendo as above*)

B "Why, that's quite alright, the money I don't mind—
It only works out about twopence a grind!"

B roars with mirth, C joins in. A looks puzzled, and eventually B sees him standing, unmoved, and his laugh dies

Singin . . .

B and C Fol-de-rum-day, fol-de-rum-day——

For once B's ebullience is dimmed. Suddenly A sees the joke and screams with laughter—

A "Twopence a grind!"

B glares at him, A realizes he is too late; all three turn to the front and half-heartedly finish the chorus without gestures

Omnes —fol-de-rum-diddle-um-diddle-um-day.

B Now, come all you young lads, (*Pointing at the audience*)

Omnes And mind what you're at. (*They also point with right index fingers*)

Don't let 'em get caught (*All three put both hands over the vital areas*)
. . . in a molecatcher's trap!
Singin . . . (*They turn right, maintaining the pose*)
Fol-de-rum-day, etc. (*They trot off* R, *still crouched and in step, keeping their faces turned to the front*)

As they go off the piano picks up the tune which is repeated for the calls and which rises a semitone after each repeat. For the calls the three yokels trot in step across the stage from R *to* L, *still singing and keeping the hunched posture with their hands cupped. If there is no exit* L *they can simply circle round the stage and make their final exit* R

For the back-announcement, the Chairman can say something appreciative, such as "thank you, gentlemen, for that gripping story" and then he should give the real names of the performers, i.e. "that was, of course, your own the Messrs A——, B——, etc. Nothing could follow that item other than the End of The World so now, as advertised, we proudly present our internationally renowned Interval, etc., etc." For interval jokes and Chairman's patter in general, see my *It Gives Me Great Pleasure* (Samuel French).

WHO WILL MAN THE LIFEBOAT?

The first production was given at the Thorndike Theatre, Leatherhead, on August 26th, 1975, with the following artistes:

Chairman	Michael Kilgarriff
1st Soprano	Joyce Rae
2nd Soprano	Jacqueline Clarke
Contralto	Stella Moray
Mariner	Barrie Gosney
Tenor	David Morton
Bass	Norman Warwick

Directed by Michael Kilgarriff

Scene—a beach
Time—summer, 1900

The cast consists of three men and three women; they can be of any age, shape or size (with the exception of the Mariner, who has to be lifted and should not, therefore, be too heavy), but they must all be able to sing and to harmonize (again with the exception of the Mariner, who sings least of all)

WHO WILL MAN THE LIFEBOAT?

Chairman With the summer holidays in mind (*adjust to suit the season*) we think of the delights afforded by the seaside . . . actually, I went in the sea myself the other day, but it didn't come up to my expectations . . . the tide was out . . . but I was so shocked! There was this very comely young girl lying on the beach and there was a hole in her bathing-costume! A hole—really, I didn't know where to put myself. Well, I mean—you could distinctly see her left knee! Anyway, where was I? Ah yes, as we disport ourselves on the sands or in the briny itself, how often do we consider those noble and hardy souls whose lives are spent sailing the oceans of the world? Whether in the merchant marine or the Royal Navy the sailor's life is a constant battle with the elements and it is only by his ceaseless endeavours that Britain stands where she does today . . . yes . . . well, we therefore now pay our humble tribute to those great-hearted men of oak who, around our country's shores, bravely and vigilantly—man the lifeboats!

There is a loud clap of thunder, the stage darkens and as the tabs open lightning flashes and the piano plays storm music. The Chairman opens up a large, striped umbrella—if the piano is on stage he can hurry across and hold it above the Pianist

Across the back of the stage is a sea groundrow; angled UR *is a bathing-tent and angled* UL *is a breakwater. Deck-chairs, lobster-pots, beach-balls, a bucket and spade, nets, etc., can be strewn about as dressing*

A cut-out of a steamer or nineteenth-century iron ship appears above the groundrow R. *It should be picked out by a follow spot. The ship battles to centre stage, then suddenly turns vertical, holds that position for a few seconds, and then slowly sinks. The follow spot closes to* BO

The thunder can die away, but the lightning can be maintained at

a reduced rate. The piano gives a bell note as the 1st Soprano appears DR

1st VERSE

1st Soprano Who will man the lifeboat, who the storm will brave?
Many souls are drifting, helpless on the wave.
See their hands uplifted, hear their bitter cry:

The 2nd Soprano and Alto appear round DR *proscenium arch or tabs*

2nd Soprano
Alto } Save us ere we perish, save us ere we die!

The 2nd Soprano and Alto come on and stand either side of the 1st Soprano; the 2nd Soprano to her R, *and Alto to her* L

1st CHORUS

Omnes Who will man the life-boat, (*with hands in praying attitude*)
Who will launch away?
Who will help to rescue (*hands at shoulder level, palms facing front*)
Dying souls today?
Who will man the life-boat, (*back to praying pose*)
Who will breast the wave?
All its dangers braving, (*hands outstretched, but not too far*)
Precious souls to save. (*hands on left bosom*)

2nd VERSE

As this verse starts, the lifeboat appears LC*; it comes on just enough for us to see two figures sitting in it, back to back, their hands shading their eyes. They should remain motionless*

Ladies	Who will man the life-boat, Who the storm will brave?	(*hands cupped in each other*)
	Many souls are drifting, Helpless on the wave.	
	See their hands uplifted,	(*ladies raise their hands to shoulder level with palms facing front; Lifeboatmen rise—still back to back—and gazing manfully*)
	Hear their bitter cry,	(*ladies put left hands to their ears, the right hand remaining in the previous position; the Lifeboatmen turn round and start slightly as they meet each other's gaze. As the Mariner begins to sing they turn to face him*)
Mariner	Save us ere we perish,	(*appearing above groundrow* C. *Follow spot on*)
	Save us ere we die!	(*disappearing below the waves. Follow spot out*)

2nd CHORUS

Lifeboat-men	We will man the lifeboat,	(*clenched fists on heart*)
{	We will launch away!	(*indicate where Mariner was last seen*)
Ladies {	Hallelujah!	(*hands to shoulder level with palms fluttering*)
Ladies	They will help to rescue,	(*indicate Lifeboatmen with left hands*)
	Dying souls today!	(*hands on bosoms*)
Lifeboat-men	We Will!	(*right index fingers firmly shaken twice*)
	We will man the life-boat,	(*clenched fists on heart*)

	We will breast the wave!	(*indicate where Mariner was last seen*)
Ladies	Hallelujah!	(*as previous Hallelujah*)
Omnes	All its dangers braving	(*ladies put hands on hearts, Lifeboatmen again shake index fingers firmly*)
Mariner	Precious souls to save!	(*rising and sinking. Follow spot on and off*)

3rd CHORUS (*sung pianissimo*)

Omnes	Who will man the life-boat, Who will launch away? Who will help to rescue, Dying souls today?	(*Omnes have their arms down by the sides*)
		(*the Mariner appears briefly agonisedly but soundlessly trying to attract attention. He sinks beneath the waves unheeded. Follow spot on and off*)
	Who will man the life-boat, Who will breast the wave? All its dangers braving, Precious souls to save!	(*the Mariner rises and sinks yet again*)

4th CHORUS (*sung fortissimo*)

Who will man the life-boat, Who will launch away? Who will help to rescue Dying souls today? Who will man the life-boat, Who will breast the wave?	(*Contralto moves across front of stage with a collecting-box, rattling it at the audience, the Chairman, pianist. On reaching* LC *she exits. 1st Soprano takes a tambourine and circles behind Contralto. She exits through bathing-tent* UR. *2nd Soprano beats a bass*

All its dangers braving,
Precious souls to save! *drum* DR *and exits there on the end of the chorus. All these props should be handed to the ladies through the* DR *opening. Simultaneously: The Lifeboatmen mime swimming to the groundrow* UC. *As they reach it the Mariner's spot appears and they lift him over the top, shake him upside down and then put him down. All three walk to the bathing-tent; the Mariner shakes hands with them and exits)*

Lifeboatmen Singing Rule, Britannia! (*standing by the bathing-tent facing front*)

Britannia Rule the waves! (*left arms to waves*)

Britons never never never (*right index fingers shake in tempo. If the man on the right has his left arm across his companion's chest, his companion's right hand can come up under it*)

Shall be slaves! (*they exit swiftly. The follow spot swings to the opposite side of the stage, as the lifeboat comes fully on*

Alto Yes, it's Rule, Britannia! *bearing the Contralto dressed*
Britannia Rule the waves! *as Britannia. As she reaches* C *a cut-out of the Royal Coat of Arms descends from the flies*)

Britons never never never (*the lifeboat starts to move off* R)

Shall . . . be . . . (*it rapidly gathers speed, to Britannia's consternation. Simultaneously: the Coat of Arms flies out*) slav—yeow! (*the boat whizzes off and we hear a yell and a crash. Follow spot* BO *as Britannia disappears*)

After a pause for applause the Lights come up to full. The Chairman can now put down his umbrella and return to his place (if he has moved) saying, with a big grin, "I think it's going to clear up, don't you?" This can lead directly into the same six artistes returning in bathing-costumes with a bright and jolly version of "Oh, I Do Like To Be Beside The Seaside" (Francis, Day, Hunter) or he can lead into the next item, which should be a straight chorus song, with a suitable link such as "I think I can guarantee us all a little sunshine now as Miss A—— B—— sings for us, etc., etc." A third alternative is for the Chairman to lead directly into the interval, e.g., "I think it's going to clear up, don't you? Well, all that excitement has made me thirsty and the Maestro could do with a quick pi . . . anissimo, I know . . . I can tell from the look on his face . . . so we'll have a break of ten minutes or so, during which time the Maestro and I will retire behind the arras, where we shall talk about you. Thank you." The Chairman bangs his gavel, blows out his candle, tabs in (if any), House Lights up and the Pianist plays one chorus of a suitable popular chorus.

The Lifeboatmen can have bathing-costumes on under their oil-skins; during the second chorus of "Rule Britannia" they can remove the oilskins and sou'westers and put on boaters and gloves. There should be a brief introduction and they enter to a chorus through the bathing-tent. They then sing the first verse, DL, with the Mariner—who has changed from rags into similar bathing attire and gloves and boater—entering through the tent as the character of Timothy. He plays the end of the verse drunk and the three of them do a repeat chorus with Timothy between them; at the end of this second chorus the Pianist needs to play an extended four-bar link into a third and final chorus, during which the girls appear in the tent door, also in bathing-costumes. All six sing a final chorus with an extended ending, and a Black-out to finish.

THE TRAM-TRACK TRAGEDY

This version, developed from an original script by Peter and Paddy Ariss of the Tower Theatre, Canonbury, was first produced at the Aba Daba Music Hall, Gray's Inn Road, London, on June 3rd, 1976, with the following cast:

Chairman	Michael Kilgarriff
Belle	Adrienne Frank
Nellie	Jacqueline Clarke
Lemuel	David Tate
Sir Putrid Canker	Johnny Dennis
Claud Body	Barrie Gosney

Directed by Michael Kilgarriff

Scene 1 Little Nellie's hovel
Scene 2 The Tram-Track

The time—1890

THE TRAM-TRACK TRAGEDY

The Chairman's table is DL, *the piano is on stage* DR. *Centre stage is a table on which lie a basket and a large wooden spoon. In the basket is a baby's blanket to make a crib. On the side of the piano is a large sign which reads:* "*LITTLE NELLIE'S HOVEL*"

Chairman (*standing* DC) My lords, ladies and gentlemen, we are now privileged to be witness to one of the most remarked dramatic offerings of the decade; I refer, of course, to that histrionic homily, that Homeric harangue, that . . . er . . . hortative . . . er . . . er . . . h'eclogue—don't you know what a h'eclogue is? (*He waits for audience response*) Well, a h'eclogue is a sort of a h'elegy . . . and is entitled: "The Tram-Track Tragedy"!

A chord of music is played

(*To the band*) Is that in it? . . . oh . . . next time take your gloves off . . . (*To the audience*) It is possible that one or two of the more delicate minded of you may find either the dialogue or some aspects of the plot to be perhaps suggestive or even indecorous; we make no apology for this, since it is our avowed intention to depict before your very glassy eyes true life as it really is . . . in the raw! (*He breathes heavily, overcome by his own vehemence. He continues, having pulled himself together*) To perform this pathetic piece we have a distinguished company of amateur tragedians who are of course so very well known in Penge and the outer suburbs (*or local district*). They are none other than the Combined Spot-Welders, Abattoir Operatives and Midden Cleaners Association Dramatic Society . . . B team. So now, it is with pride, a stiff upper lip and fallen arches, that I now announce: "The Tram-Track Tragedy", or, "Little Nellie's Bloomers"!

He retires to his table DL *and sits*

Music plays and Belle enters from out front or from UR. *She is sister to the heroine and so must appear to possess all the virtues; we can possibly detect a certain tartiness in her make-up, however, and with Lemuel, in the final scene, she becomes positively brazen. But her heart is in the right place and she is well spoken*

Belle Alas, alas, that my sister Nell and I should have fallen so low . . . (*she trips but recovers*) to be cold and starving in this . . . er . . . (*She appears to dry*)

The Chairman and the Pianist draw her attention to the sign

. . . Little Nellie's Hovel. We have not so much as one farthing left with which to buy food for ourselves or for Nell's little baby, Willie. Would that Dame Fortune would smile upon us once again as she did in days of yore. But see—my dear sister comes!

Belle clears to L *of table*

Pathetic music—"Hearts and Flowers"?—and Nellie enters, either from out front or from UL. *She has a shawl over her head and is carrying little Willie wrapped in a blanket. She is slighter and younger than Belle, and has not had the same educational advantages as her sister in that her accent is decidedly proletarian. She is also more than a trifle stupid but is by no means devoid of charm*

Nellie Oh, this horrible hovel!
Belle Sister mine, where have you been all these long, weary hours?
Nellie (*to* R *of the table*) I have been walking the streets . . .
Belle (*shocked, but envious*) Oh!
Nellie In search of food . . .
Belle Oh . . .
Nellie Without success.
Belle Alas, alas. And how fares the child?
Nellie Half fare—he's still under age . . . (*The penny drops. Laughing*) Oh! . . . No—not well, I fear! (*Her expression changes instantly to high drama*) Poor mite, he too is cold and hungry,

with not even a cradle to sleep in. (*Putting the baby in the basket on the table*) Just a little basket . . . poor little Willie.
Belle (*opening the swaddling clothes*) Yes, *such* a little Willie . . .

They both trip daintily, one on each side of the table, to below it DC

Sister dear, I have a good friend—only the widow of a poor bookmaker, 'tis true—but she will not deny me a crust of bread, I am sure. To her hence hopefully will I hie me hither.

They both turn outwards and trip daintily above the table to UC

Nellie (*now on Belle's* R) You are so good to me, Belle. Long may you be by my side.
Belle Just hang on to Belle, Nellie. Hang on to Belle.

Belle exits UR

The Chairman displays a sign, "Hooray"

The piano plays a chord and Belle re-enters to take a sweeping call, after which she finally exits

Nellie (*during this speech she can make a complete circuit of the stage, but she must finish by the* UL *exit*) Dear, kind sister . . . but 'tis well she has gone, for I am shortly expecting . . . (*she has a momentary dry*) . . . the arrival of the one who has enslaved my affections, who has captured my heart. Yes, the father of my child! If only he would marry me . . . if only the proud, haughty Sir Putrid Canker would give me his name and proclaim it to the world so that I might not have to hobble about this horrible hovel and grovel . . . but soft, 'tis he!

Lemuel enters immediately, close to her L

Lemuel (*his accent is thick and vaguely Transylvanian*) 'Tis not!
Nellie 'Tis who?
Lemuel 'Tis me.
Nellie But 'tis-who *are* 'tis-you?
Lemuel I am Lemuel the Gypsy . . . but you can call me . . .

(*moving* DL) . . . Lemuel. (*This is said slowly and with great relish*)

Nellie (*to his* R) What is your business with me, Romany sir?

Lemuel Cross my palm with silver, pretty lady, and I shall reveal to you the secrets of the future.

Nellie Alas, everything I had to give I have already given.

Lemuel Everything?

Nellie (*shamefully indicating the basket with her head*) Everything.

Lemuel moves above her to above the table and opens the baby's wrappings

I should dearly love to know what is written in the stars for my little son.

Lemuel (*who has now seen the face and has reacted with horror*) Aaagh! It can't be . . .! (*He peers again more closely but the hideousness of the baby is too much for him*) Aaaagh! It can't be . . .!

Nellie (*quite unoffended*) I assure you he is my own son.

Lemuel (*moving* DRC. *Behind his hand*) This infant is the image of Sir Putrid Canker, the betrayer of my own dear daughter and the scourge of my tribe . . . so he has ruined this unfortunate lady, too, has he . . .? (*He moves in to below the table. Aloud*) Give me your hand, my dear.

Nellie Why, what are you going to do with it?

Lemuel Divine your destiny . . . (*He takes her proffered hand*)

Nellie (*slightly disappointed*) Oh . . .

Lemuel (*with his face very close to her palm*) What's this . . .? Yes, just as I thought.

Nellie What?

Lemuel Strawberry jam. (*He licks her palm*) Yes, yes . . . no, no . . . yes, yes . . .

Nellie What can you see now?

Lemuel I see a man . . . a man with evil designs . . .

Nellie Oh!

Lemuel (*he lets her hand go and moves* DR) Beware this dastard!

Nellie Who can he be? (*She moves* DL)

Lemuel (*slyly pulling his shirt open to reveal one nipple. Aside*) I dare not reveal any more . . . (*Aloud*) His name your palm does not reveal, but you are to meet him very soon. (*He moves to* UL *exit above the table*)

Nellie I am?

Lemuel You are. There is definitely a date in your palm. Beware!

Lemuel exits

The Chairman again displays the "Hooray" sign

Lemuel re-enters and takes an elaborate call to suitable chords from the piano, after which he finally exits

Nellie (*looking at her hand*) How strange . . . the only gentleman who knows of my existence here is Sir Putrid, and he would do me no harm, I am sure, for he loves me . . . (*during this she takes off her shawl and puts it on the table*) . . . as you will shortly discover! (*She moves* DL *and adjusts her hair in an imaginary mirror*)

The music turns "villainous", the Lights lower, and a green follow spot picks out the figure of Sir Putrid slowly appearing from the UR *entrance. As his face comes into view his eyes slither about the stage, and then do a double-take on Nellie. He slowly walks to the* DR *corner of the table. He is of indeterminate age, but his voice and deportment are those of a Regency fop. He is immensely fastidious with a high, affected voice*

Sir Putrid Ah, Nellie, me dear . . . how nice to find ye here . . . alone . . .

Nellie (*moving below the table* C) Oh, Sir Putrid, have pity on me and on our child . . . our ailing little child, to whom I have given suck.

Sir Putrid (*crossing her to* LC) Spare me the anatomical reminiscences, woman.

Nellie See how ill he is . . . so wan.

Sir Putrid (*aside*) Better wan than two . . . (*Aloud. Moving in to Nellie*) What is it ye want from me, slut?

Nellie Oh, Sir Putrid, I wish to plead my cause.

Sir Putrid (*aside*) The miserable pleader.

Nellie (*kneeling and grasping him round the right leg*) Marry me and acknowledge the child as your heir.
Sir Putrid (*turning*) What?

He attempts to pull his leg away but Nellie pulls it back

Nev . . . (*He tries again*) Nev . . .

He tries a third time. She lets go and he hurts his thigh

Oooo! Never!
Nellie Marry me or I will bruit it from the housetops that you are the progenitor of that ailing little babe to whom I have given suck!
Sir Putrid I knew I'd have trouble with that little sucker. (*Crossing* DR) Very well, Nell, me dear. I'll take ye to the altar—on the morrow!
Nellie (*rising*) Oh!
Sir Putrid We elope—tonight!
Nellie (*moving* DLC) Rapture!
Sir Putrid (*aside*) This is me chance to be rid of her and the brat for once and for all . . . (*Aloud. Moving to* R *of the table*) Meet me at midnight, my love, and bring our boy with ye. (*He glances in the basket and reacts at the baby*) Strewth . . .!
Nellie And where shall we meet?
Sir Putrid At Paddington Green. By the old—tram-track!

A piano chord is struck

(*Moving to Nellie's* R) Now, go and make ready for a very long journey.
Nellie Oh, I do love experiencing foreign parts!

She blows him a kiss and exits behind him UR, *ecstatically*

The Chairman again displays the "Hooray" sign

Nellie re-enters and she takes a call, after which she finally exits

Sir Putrid (*moving* DL) Ugh, how unattractive she seems to me now . . . how could I ever have wanted to stir her cocoa . . .? Me plan cannot fail . . . (*Crossing to* DR) By daybreak I'll see Willy chilly and Nellie jelly . . . (*approaching the basket*) . . . now might I do it pat . . . (*stretching out his hands*) . . . shall I?

The Chairman displays a "No!" sign

You lily-livered lot of milk-sops! (*Moving to* UC *above the table*) May your noses all drop off!

He exits

He moves UL *then takes a scowling call as the Chairman displays a "Boo!" sign, after which Sir Putrid finally exits*

The piano plays heroic music as we hear the voice of Claud Body off

Claud also enters either from out front or from either of the downstage entrances—or from UL *if this is the only practical entrance available. He is very short and has poor eyesight. Nor is he too convincing an actor, delivering his lines rather flatly and woodenly. But he is very sincere and not a bit nervous, giving him considerable strength and pace. He is carrying an assegai and wears a rucksack hung about with comedy props—a hot-water bottle, chamber-pot, saucepan, child's bucket and spade, etc., etc.*

Claud (*as he enters*) Nellie! My Nellie! Are you at home? I'm back . . . from Africa! (*He is now on stage* DC)

Nellie enters UR, *and crosses to* DL *without seeing him*

Nellie That voice . . .! Can it be . . . Claud?
Claud It can be and it is! Your faithful and devoted childhood sweetheart, now a famous big-game hunter, Claud Body. (*He moves* DR *and leans his assegai against the piano or any available piece of scenery; if there is none, a hand can come from the wings and take it*)
Nellie Claud!
Claud Nellie!

They run to each other and embrace DC. *Nellie reacts with pain and moves back a pace*

(*Indicating the water-bottle, which is slung from his belt like a sporran*) Sorry, my love, my cork's come out. (*He replaces the cork and then goes* RC *and takes off his rucksack, placing it on the floor behind the piano or against the* R *drapes*)

Nellie So you are a big-game hunter, are you?
Claud Yes, my dear. (*He has been fiddling with the rucksack with his back to the audience. Now he turns with a piece of feathery trimming in his hand*) See, I've brought you back a little furry denizen of the jungle as a present.
Nellie Oh!
Claud It's perfectly harmless. It only wakes up at night.

The "denizen" leaps out of his hand and runs around the set, disappearing from view near the Chairman, who dives out of his chair in terror

Must be past his bedtime.

He and Nellie chat together, she having come to him

Sir Putrid pokes his head round the UL *entrance*

Sir Putrid This poltroon threatens to foil me carefully laid scheme . . . I must get rid of him—I know! I'll send him a bogus message recalling him to the jungle . . . yes . . . I'll send it by Bush Telegraph!

He disappears with an evil laugh

Claud (*crossing Nellie to above the table*) And now, my darling, I claim you as my bride—aagh! (*He sees the baby and is appalled*) But what is this?
Nellie (*thinking quickly as she moves across below the table to* DLC) Er . . . this is my child, Claud . . . *our* son.
Claud Oh . . . I've been away three years, Nellie.
Nellie But you wrote such lovely letters, Claud.
Claud (*reassured*) Little Nellie, embrace your passionate Body.

He opens his arms, closes his eyes and waits for her as Lemuel enters, lightly disguised as a messenger boy

Lemuel (*speaking very effeminately*) Express message for Mr Claud Body the famous African explorer——

Claud inadvertently has embraced him

(*Wincing*) Oh . . .!

Claud (*almost sotto voce. Indicating his water-bottle*) Sorry about that—it's just my water-bottle . . . (*Crossing above the table to* LC) I am Body. Give me the message.

Lemuel (R *of the table. Aside, and speaking as Lemuel*) I'll seem to help along Sir Putrid's plans, thus to ensure his downfall. (*Aloud, as messenger boy*) The message, sir? Certainly. (*He reaches under the table and pulls out a tom-tom which he beats rhythmically for a few seconds as Claud listens intently*)

Claud (*nodding*) Mmmmm . . . no reply.

Lemuel holds out his hand for a tip, and Claud shakes it. Claud returns to Nellie as Lemuel catches sight of the baby in the basket, he reacts with a squeal

Lemuel exits UL

Nellie What was the message?

Claud My dear, I have to return to Africa on the evening tide.

They embrace LC

Nellie So soon? After three years away from me?

Claud Yes, my dear. It's very hard.

Nellie's rump shifts away from him slightly

Nellie But why must you go?

Claud Some chap has got himself lost in the jungle. (*He goes across to put his rucksack back on—this time back to front—and to collect his assegai*) It's Livingstone, I presume. Confound these amateurs . . . anyway, Her Majesty—(*he raises his pith helmet respectfully*)—has graciously commanded me to go and look for him. (*He is now* DC *if he is to exit through the auditorium, or* UC *if he is to exit into the wings*)

Nellie Don't forget to write, my love.

Claud I dare not do that, my angel.
Nellie Why not?
Claud I might give you the Willies!

He exits either UL *or out front or through whichever entrance he first appeared. Nellie blows him a kiss, crossing to* DR *of the table. The Chairman shows the "Hooray!" sign and as soon as the audience react he turns it over to show "Boo!" on the other side as Sir Putrid enters* UL

Sir Putrid Dearest Nellie!
Nellie Oh, Sir Putrid!

Sir Putrid moves to below the table and shows her a bottle marked "Poison" and with a skull and crossbones

Sir Putrid See what I have brought for our poor ailing little son . . . a soothing medicament . . . a panacea for *all* ills . . . give him a big spoonful.

They both go to above the table, one each side

Nellie Oh, thank you, I will. Indeed I will.

She picks up the wooden spoon as Sir Putrid uncorks or unscrews the bottle. He pours some poison on to the spoon and Nellie gives it to the baby

There you are, my little cherub. Isn't it kind of Daddikins?

Sir Putrid adlibs inanities to the baby, peering closely at the baby

Sir Putrid There's a good boy. Enjoy your medicine——

The baby spits a stream of liquid into Sir Putrid's face

Nellie Oh, don't be such a silly billy, Willie . . . there, see? He is sleeping already.

Belle enters, unseen, UL

Sir Putrid And you will meet me tonight as arranged, at the old tram-track?
Nellie (*nodding*) Paddington Green.
Sir Putrid On the stroke of midnight.

Belle (*over his* L *shoulder*) When?
Sir Putrid (*involuntarily*) Midnight.

Belle nips off UR

Sir Putrid double-takes, looking off UL *as though not too sure what has happened*

Nellie I shall be there, never fear.
Sir Putrid (*moving to* DC) Don't forget your bag. You're going on a long trip.
Nellie (*moving to his* R) Have you ever been abroad?
Sir Putrid Frequently, but tonight I'm a chap . . . that's a joke . . . I don't make 'em often so enjoy it while you can.

Nellie gives the minutest and faintest of laughs

Enough! (*He goes swiftly to the* UL *entrance and turns on his heels*) Just one thing!
Nellie (*jumping*) Oh!
Sir Putrid Give Willie some more medicine . . . just to make sure.
Nellie (*going to above the table*) Very well . . . (*Looking into the basket*) Oh! He is convulsed.
Sir Putrid (*at her* L) Is he? He's on his own—(*indicating a section of the audience*)—there's not a titter down here.
Nellie (*her big moment*) Oh, oh, oh! Too late! He is dead, dead—and never——
Nellie / **Sir Putrid** } —called me Mother! { (*Speaking together*)
Sir Putrid Yes, we know—get on with it.
Nellie Oh, Willie, my darling child! (*She swoons gracefully and carefully to the floor to the* R *of the table*)
Putrid There's more ham in here than on a bacon counter. (*Looking in the basket*) Yes, the brat has expired. (*Mock tragic*) Dead, dead—and never called me Daddy!

He laughs evilly and exits UL. *Belle enters* UR, *looking off* L

Belle Was that the man from the Pru? (*She sees Nellie*) Oh, my poor sister? (*She kneels by her*) Nell, it's Belle! Aren't you well? (*She rises*) Oh, isn't it hell to dwell in this fell cell . . . (*She looks into the basket*) But Willie . . . (*She opens the blanket*) So limp and white . . . (*She closes the blanket. She sees the poison bottle on the table*) And what's this? "Poison". (*She turns it over*) "Property of Sir Putrid Canker" . . . this could be a clue! My suspicions are aroused . . . (*Moving to* DLC) . . . where was it Nellie and Sir Putrid arranged to meet? At the old tram-track at midnight . . . to thwart Sir Putrid's plot, whatever it may be. I shall keep this sinister tryst in my sister's stead. (*She wipes her mouth after all those juicy sibilants, or, alternatively, she can apologise briefly to the front row for splashing them*) I shall wear her shawl—(*she takes it from the table and puts it on*)—and shall now wend my fearful way to Paddington Green!

She exits UR, *having to leap daintily over Nellie's body en route*

The Chairman displays the "Hooray!" sign

Belle re-enters and takes her call, after which she finally exits

The follow spot is switched off as the Chairman then moves to the table C

Chairman (*to Nellie*) All right, gal.

Nellie rises very matter-of-factly, takes the basket, and exits UR

(*Moving back with the table*) It's going well, isn't it?

He moves into the wings L *as the Pianist turns over the sign on the piano to reveal "Danger—Tram-Track" on the reverse, plus a severed hand pointing to the stage* C. *The Chairman then sits in his chair and the Lights lower*

There is a moment's silence and then an alarm clock is heard shrilling loudly for six seconds. It cuts off abruptly and Sir Putrid's evil face peers round the UL *entrance*

Sir Putrid Midnight . . .! And all is deserted . . . (*coming* DLC) . . .

like Aberdeen on a flag-day . . . Me plan goes well . . . (*moving* UC *and looking off* R) . . . she approaches! Ha, ha, ha! (*He moves* DC) A lamb to the slaughter!

Belle enters with the shawl over her head. She is holding it as a shield across her face with her left hand, in which she is also carrying the poison bottle. She comes to C

Sweet Nellie, me heart's desire . . . (*he takes the bottle and puts it in his pocket*) . . . and you've returned me empty, how thoughtful . . . nothing to say, for once?

Belle shakes her head

(*Moving* DL) Too overcome with emotion, no doubt. (*Aside*) I've always had that effect on the fair sex. (*Moving back to her* L) Now, me pretty, you are in me grasp! (*He grabs her with one hand and produces a length of rope in the other. He pulls her down so that she is lying sideways on the stage on one elbow, facing the audience; he then mimes tying her hands to the tram-track behind her*) Struggle as ye may, 'twill avail ye naught. I'll tie ye to the track and the noise of the midnight tram will cover your screams. (*He stands*) Your doom is sealed!

He exits UL *in triumph*

Belle Help! Help!

As Sir Putrid exits the Chairman displays the "Boo!" sign; immediately the audience reacts he turns it over to show the "Hooray!" as Claud enters

Claud enters either from out front or from where he last went off

Claud Did I hear a cry for help?
Belle Here, oh quickly, here!

Claud wanders around the stage, stepping over Belle

Claud I wonder where it can be coming from . . . I can't see a thing in this darkness . . .

Belle Here, Claud!
Claud (*on her* R) Why, Nellie—Bellie—Belle! What are you doing here?
Belle I'm tied to the tram-track, Claud. Cut me free, quick!
Claud Of course, with my rusty—trusty knife! (*He takes out his sheath-knife, drops to his knees and begins sawing at the rope behind Belle's back*)
Belle Hurry! Hurry!

The Lights lower and a flickering follow spot picks out a small painted cardboard cut-out of a tram moving across the back of the stage from L *to* R, *about five feet from the floor. The driver is seen in silhouette to be wearing a peaked cap and a ginger beard. As the tram disappears the flicker-light stops and the stage Lights momentarily come up*

Quick—it's getting closer!

Again the Lights go down and the flicker-spot picks out another tram cut-out, this one three times larger, travelling across the stage at the same height but in the opposite direction. There is, of course, suitable dramatic flurrying music. The second tram disappears into the wings, L. *The Lights come up and Claud rises*

Claud The last rope is cut!
Belle (*also rising*) Saved!

The Chairman shows the "Hooray!" sign as Lemuel enters UL, *stepping down on to the stage as though from the platform of a tram. He is wearing a heavy overcoat, a ginger beard and a peaked cap over his red head-scarf*

Lemuel (*in a non-Lemuel accent*) You all right, miss?
Belle (*moving to* C) Thank goodness the midnight train was late. And thank you for stopping, driver.
Lemuel Nay, miss. Thank . . .

With a tremendous flourish he tears off the overcoat and hands it to the Chairman, who has approached him as inconspicuously as possible. He also removes the beard and the cap and hands them to the Chairman

. . . Lemuel the Gypsy! (*He now speaks in his original Lemuel accent*) I am indeed late, for I had to foil my conductor.

Lemuel indicates L *as the Conductor, enveloped in a black cloak and wearing a peaked cap, enters* UL, *also as though stepping off a tram*

Belle But why?
Lemuel He was a lightning conductor . . . but known to Society as . . .

The Chairman whips off the Conductor's cloak and peaked cap, and Lemuel slaps a villainous moustache on his face as he puts on his own top hat

. . . Sir Putrid Canker!

There is general sensation. The Chairman retires to his table

Nellie enters UR *with the baby*

Belle is now DR, *Claud* RC, *Lemuel* LC *and Sir Putrid* DL, *but all are quite close together, leaving just a gap* C *for Nellie*

Nellie Oh, Sir Putrid, there you are. I trust I am not too late for our tryst? Willie is well after all. He was merely in a cataleptic trance and wanted winding. Why—(*turning to each in turn*)—Belle . . . Lemuel . . . Claud . . . what is the reason for this untoward assemblage?
Lemuel I believe I can explain all. I am not a tram-driver, nor even, as I had led you to believe, a gypsy. My name is in fact . . .

Again he and the Chairman spring into action. Lemuel whips off his headscarf and ear-ring and hands them to the Chairman, who gives him first a deerstalker hat which he dons, and then a magnifying-glass and a meerschaum pipe

. . . Hawkshaw! (*This new identity is delivered in standard P.C. Plod tones*)

Belle Hawkshaw the detective?
Lemuel The very same.
Nellie Not Hawkshaw of the Inch?

Lemuel Of the Yard.

Belle
Nellie } Oooohmmmmm! { (*Together*)

Nellie (*moving to Claud's* L) But what brings you to this dismal scene, Claud?

Claud I was just passing by chance, having missed the boat.

Sir Putrid (*addressing Claud and moving* C) One moment, sir. I perceive a watch-chain of a singular design across your person. You observe that I have an identical one?

They both stand C *in profile to the audience, quite close together and fingering their fobs*

Claud Mine's bigger than yours . . . but they do indeed have the same design.

Sir Putrid You know what this indicates?

Claud You don't mean?

Sir Putrid Yes! That you are my long-lost twin brother!

This creates a sensation

Claud Puty!

Sir Putrid Claud!

They embrace, and Sir Putrid is prodded painfully by the water-bottle

Claud Sorry about that . . .

Sir Putrid (*recovering*) But you are my elder by ten minutes, so you must now assume the title. You are the rightful baronet!

This creates another sensation. Nellie crosses to Claud's L

Henceforth I shall lead a life of purity and good works, and shall repent the error of my ways.

Lemuel In that case all charges will be dropped.

Belle (*sauntering over to Lemuel's* R) How can I thank you, Hawkshaw of the . . . Yard?

Lemuel By placing yourself in my custody . . . for life.

She takes his arm happily

Sir Putrid Let us all repair to Canker Castle for a celebration. I have something very special in me wine cellar for just such an occasion . . .

Omnes Oooh, yes! (*Etc., ad-libitum*)
Sir Putrid A very memorable cordial . . .
Omnes *Oooh!*
Sir Putrid You'll never taste anything better . . .
Omnes OOOH!
Sir Putrid Ever . . .
Claud Ripping! We'd love to come, wouldn't we?
Omnes Yes, rather! (*Etc., ad-libitum*)
Sir Putrid And furthermore, to atone for me past misdeeds, I shall return to me old calling—(*he rips off his shirt-front, which comes away in one piece with the cravat, revealing a clerical collar and black stock*)—the Ministry!
Nellie You mean . . . ?
Sir Putrid Yes! 'Twas all a clerical error!

A bell note is sounded from the piano

(*Singing to the tune of* "*For He Is An Englishman*" *from* "*H.M.S. Pinafore*") For I am a clergyman! (*Speaking*) C. of E., of course.

Omnes (*singing*) For he himself has said it,
And it's greatly to his credit,
That he is an Anglican!
Sir Putrid Yes, a High Church Anglican!
Claud Not a follower of Johnny Knox,
Belle Nor Greek,
Nellie Nor Russian
Belle, Nellie Orthodox!
Lemuel Nor Episcopalian!
Omnes Nor Episcopalian!
No, in spite of all temptations,
To belong to strange persuasions,
He remains an Anglican,
He remains an Anglican!

Sir Putrid (*speaking*) The fools!
Omnes (*speaking*) Hurrah!
Sir Putrid (*speaking*) The fools! (*He gets out the poison bottle*)
Omnes (*speaking*) Hurrah!
Sir Putrid (*speaking*) The fools!
Omnes (*speaking*) Hurrah!

Sir Putrid The fools!
Omnes (*singing*) Hurrah!

They all bow as the Chairman shows a sign reading "The End". The music reprises "For I Am An Anglican"

Nellie and Claud exit, then Belle and Lemuel, leaving Sir Putrid stroking the poison bottle and gloating

A three-second fade to BO. *No further calls should be necessary.* (*The Cast can exit through any of the available exits, or out front, as long as they all go the same way.*) *The Chairman then moves to* C

Chairman Ladies and gentlemen, I am not easily moved . . . but during that performance I very nearly went . . . (*He then gives the names of the Cast if they are not listed in the programme*) So now, to enable you to ingest both the moral of the tale and anything which may be on sale for ready cash at the rear of the auditorium, we now proudly present our internationally renowned *interval*!!! (*He bangs his gavel and blows out his candle*)

The stage Lights go down, the house Lights come up, and the piano plays a chorus of "Riding On Top Of The Car" (Francis, Day & Hunter for the entr'acte)

THE MASTER AND THE MAID

The setting is a simple box-set interior of the 1900 period. There is a door L *and a door* R*; the only essential piece of furniture is a table* DR *on which rests the Wife's hat and her parasol (or handbag). Drapes, of course, are perfectly acceptable if a full box-set is not practical for such a short sketch*

Chairman Ladies and gentlemen, the management, ever straining after novelties to divert you, is now enrup—enraptured to present, for the first time in (*local place*) a demonstration of the new French invention . . . known as the Kinematograph, a device which projects actual moving pictures on to a screen!

Shouts of "No!" from out front

I assure you, sir, such is the case. I have, therefore, the singular privilege of now presenting an animated picture of that celebrated classic drama, "The Master And The Maid". Is the projectionist ready?

A shout comes from the back: "Yes!"

Very well, ladies take hold of your hankies, and gentlemen take hold of your ladies, as we present, "The Master And The Maid"!

The Lights go down to a Black-out for a couple of seconds. Then the CURTAINS*—if any—open and a flickering line, reminiscent of an early "flick", illuminates the scene. We also hear the whirring of an antique projector and ad lib piano accompaniment throughout*

1. Enter Husband L. He moves to C, straightening his tie. He is followed by his Wife, who is carrying his topper; she moves to his L.
2. The Maid enters L carrying the Husband's overcoat; she moves to R and slightly above the Husband preparatory to helping him on with his coat.

Meanwhile, Husband checks that there is a hanky up his right sleeve. He inadvertently drops it on to the floor, raises his L arm in mock surprise, then turns to his Wife and both laugh. He picks up the handkerchief and stuffs it up his R sleeve.

3. The Maid helps the Husband on with his coat and the Wife hands the Husband his topper, which he dons. He then adjusts his appearance carefully and minutely in an imaginary mirror, facing out front.
   The Maid goes to the door R and opens it.
4. The Husband pecks his Wife on the cheek and moves to the door R. The Wife moves to the table DL to begin putting on her hat.
5. The Maid curtsies and as the Husband crosses her he pinches her bottom. The Maid starts, causing the Wife to swing round to face them suspiciously. The Maid converts the scream into a cough.
6. The Husband and Wife blow kisses at each other, and the Husband exits. The Maid closes the door and moves to C.
7. The Wife now has her hat on; she picks up her parasol (or handbag) and moves to the Maid's L, upbraiding her. She then exits L.
8. The Maid thumbs her nose off after the Wife, then reacts to a knock on the door R. She opens the door and admits the Wife's Lover.
9. The Lover looks round carefully, then chucks the Maid under the chin.
10. The Wife enters L and crossly dismisses the Maid, who exits L, waving to the Lover when she has passed the Wife.
11. The Lover attempts to return the wave, but the Wife has moved to C and has opened her arms. He smothers the wave and goes to her. They embrace passionately, and then exit L.
12. After a very brief pause the Husband re-enters R very slowly. The Maid re-enters L with a feather duster, dusting. Husband calls her name and she turns to him, startled, and the duster flies out of her hand through the door L.

13. The Husband and the Maid then run into each other's arms C and kiss passionately.
14. The Wife enters L, the Husband and Maid spring apart, the Maid C and the Husband on her R. The Wife comes to the Maid's L, remonstrating bitterly.
15. The Maid, piqued, tells the Husband that the Wife's Lover is in the house; the Wife, embarrassed, moves DL. The Husband makes for the door L and the Maid moves DR.
16. The Husband reaches off L and pulls on the Lover by his R ear. When they reach C (the Husband is on the R and the Lover is on the L) they square up to each other and jig around in a semi-circle, clockwise. The Wife reacts with horror but the Maid encourages them. When the Husband is on the L and the Lover on the R, the Lover shoots out a straight left to the Husband's jaw. The Husband sags to the floor, out cold.
17. The wife immediately rushes and kneels on her Husband's L, while the Lover joins the Maid DR, she feeling his biceps admiringly.
18. The Wife helps her Husband to his feet and leads him to L exit, as the Maid leads the Lover to R exit.
19. Both women exit simultaneously, and just as the men exit they pause, turn to each other and wink. Then they exit as the Lights BO.

The piano ad lib accompaniment stops

A Light comes up on the Chairman

Chairman Did you enjoy that . . .? Jolly exciting, wasn't it . . .? A bit naughty, though . . . but would you like to see it again—no extra charge . . .?

Shouts of "Yes!" from the audience

You would . . .? Very well, but our projectionist has to run the film back first, so may we claim your indulgence while this is done. (*Calling to the rear*) Very well, monsieur . . . reversez-vous!

The Chairman's Light goes out and after a few seconds the flicker-lime is seen again

19. The Husband and Wife enter backwards L (Husband first) as the Lover and the Maid enter R, also backwards. The Husband and the Lover wink to each other, then all four come right on stage.
18. The Lover pulls the Maid backwards to DR as the groggy Husband pulls the Wife to DC where the Husband sags to the ground.
17. The Maid feels the Lover's biceps admiringly as the Wife kneels by her Husband and tries to revive him. The Wife rises and rushes backwards to DL as the Lover backs to RC, turning to face the Husband.
16. The Husband rises unsteadily to his feet, raises his fists and faces the Lover. The Lover puts out his left fist and the Husband deliberately smacks his jaw against it with a sideways swipe and a grimace of pain. Then he straightens up, very spry and chipper, jigging up and down. The Lover pulls back his left fist and also jigs up and down. Both jig round in a semi-circle anti-clockwise, then, when the Husband is R and the Lover is L, the Husband stretches out his left arm and the Lover bends and places his R ear in the Husband's left hand. The Lover is now in great pain but unaccountably drags the Husband to exit L, where the Husband releases him.
15. The Husband angrily backs DRC as the Maid backs to C. The Wife, embarrassed, backs to C as the Maid tells the Husband the Lover is in the house.
14. The Wife remonstrates bitterly with the Maid, however, then backs away L as the Maid and Husband spring into each other's arms C. The Wife backs out L with an expression of shock and surprise which changes to one of blandness just as she exits.
13. The Husband and the Maid break their clinch then back rapidly away from each other, the Maid to the L entrance and the Husband to the R entrance.
12. The Maid looks surprised, raising her R hand to her mouth and looking out front. Her L hand rises in a gesture of surprise and the feather duster comes through the L entrance into it. As the Husband calls to her, her R hand is lowered, her expression of surprise becomes one of unconcern as she dusts and backs off L.

The Husband then backs off R very slowly, shutting the door.

11. The Lover and the Wife enter L (in that order) backwards to C where they embrace passionately. The Wife releases the Lover, who then backs to the R exit, opens the door and both look furtively in either direction. The Lover smothers a wave as the Maid backs on L to LC. The Lover then smothers a wave as she turns, but the Wife is unconcerned for she turns to face the Maid, allowing the Lover to wave to the Maid cheerfully.
10. The Maid waves back then backs past the Wife to the door R. The Wife crossly dismisses her, but then inexplicably backs off L herself.
9. The Lover chucks the Maid under the chin, and then looks round carefully.
8. The Lover backs out R and the Maid shuts the door. She then backs C and turns to face L with a start of surprise. The surprise vanishes as she thumbs her nose off L.
7. The Wife backs on, with hat and parasol, to the Maid's L and upbraids her. She then backs to the table DR on which she places her parasol and begins to remove her hat.
6. The Maid backs to the door R, opens it and admits the Husband, backwards. He turns and blows kisses to the Wife, who returns them.
5. The Maid coughs, the Wife looks suspiciously but swings round to face out L—still attending to her hat. The Husband backs on stage across the Maid, she starts and he pinches her bottom.
4. Wife has now put her hat on the table DL. She backs to C as the Husband also backs to C, they turn and give each other a peck on the cheek.
3. The Maid shuts the door and backs DRC. The Husband adjusts his appearance minutely in an imaginary mirror, facing out front, paying particular attention to the angle of his topper. When it is to his satisfaction, he briskly removes it and hands it to his wife. He then smooths the collar of his coat and adjusts it set; when he removes it, helped by the Maid.
2. The Husband removes the handkerchief from his sleeve

and puts it down with his R hand on the floor. He rises, turns to the Wife, they both laugh. He puts his L arm up in the air in mock dismay and the handkerchief leaps into his R hand. He stuffs it back into his R sleeve.
The Maid backs off L with his overcoat.

1. The Wife, carrying topper, backs off L. The Husband, straightening his tie, also backs off L.

Black-out

A Light comes up on the Chairman

Chairman Well, well . . . a truly remarkable demonstration of Victorian scientific achievement at its best. We told you that you would be able to see this marvel once again, and so you shall, but we are rather pressed for time—(*glancing at his pocket-watch*)—so I will ask our projectionist to run the reel through as fast as he can. (*Calling*) Er . . . vite, monsieur, silver plate . . . Chop chop . . .

Again the Lights go down to a Black-out for a couple of seconds. The flicker-lime comes on again and the piano plays with suitable variations of pace

1.–15. These sections are performed at breakneck speed.
16. This section begins at full speed but then slows to normal, to extreme slow motion, and finally the actors freeze just as the Lover's fist connects with the Husband's jaw.

A Light comes up on the Chairman

Chairman Monsieur! Vite, vite! Je vous en prie—allez!
Voice from the Rear (*in a heavy French accent*) Sacre bleu! My sprocket, she is—'ow you say?—cloggèd. (*Pronouced with two syllables*)
A Voice Well, please unclog yourself, monsieur, and get on with it!
The Light on the Chairman goes out

16.–19. The rest of the Mime play is enacted at breakneck speed.

Calls should be taken with the flicker-lime still going. The Cast enter the line-up hand in hand and bow. They take a pace to the L, *preparatory to going off; but then suddenly they turn back to the audience and bow again. This business—i.e. as though the film is caught in a loop—is repeated ad lib until the* CURTAINS *come in; or, if you have no curtains, another Black-out. If your Black-out is not very effective it is better to cut this final gag and just have your Cast walking off after taking a bow*

Normal stage lighting comes on

Chairman What *will* they think of next . . . ? It'll never catch on . . . This was the Cast, in descending order of height . . . (*He then lists the Cast taking part*)

FURNITURE AND PROPERTY LIST

THE MOLECATCHER

Nil.

WHO WILL MAN THE LIFEBOAT?

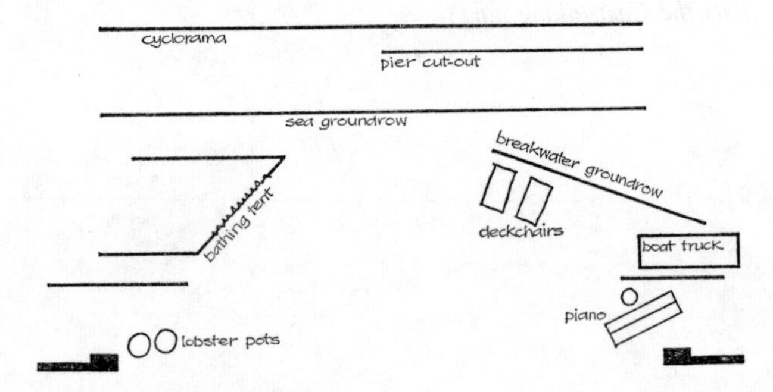

Off stage: Striped umbrella (L or R)
Collecting-box (DR)
Bass drum and stick (DR)
Tambourine (DR)
Steamer cut-out (UL or UR)
Crash bucket (RC)
Britannia's spear and shield attached to L of boat truck's bulwarks

THE TRAM-TRACK TRAGEDY

Set: Whiffenpoof. Swanee whistle can be worked by **Sir Putrid** off L
Trams: small one to move from L to R; large one to move from R to L
Chair or stool by UL entrance

Back stage: Alarm clock, tram bell (optional)—*or can be worked by the* **Chairman**

On stage: *On table* C: Shabby cloth, basket containing blanket and water-filled enema, large wooden spoon
Under table C: Tom-tom underneath, concealed by the cloth
On Chairman's table: Magnifying-glass, meerschaum pipe and deerstalker hat **(Lemuel)**
Set on prop table L:
Messenger's hat, ginger beard, long overcoat, peaked cap **(Lemuel)**
Black cloak, poison bottle, rope (4 ft. in length), peaked cap, Swanee whistle **(Sir Putrid)**
By Chairman's chair: Placards: "Hooray!"/"Boo!" and "No!"/"The End"
On side of piano (or wherever preferred): Placard: "Little Nellie's Hovel"/"Danger—Tram-Track ☛"

Personal: Assegai, rucksack (stuffed with paper and adorned with chamber-pot, hot-water bottle, frying-pan, etc.), army water-bottle on belt, watch-chain and fob, sheath-knife on belt **(Claud)**
Watch-chain and fob **(Sir Putrid)**

The watch-chains can be two cheap necklaces and the fobs any curious-shaped piece of metal or plastic—as long as they are large enough and distinctive enough to be seen (the author used two of his small daughter's hair "bobbles"!).

The whiffenpoof consists of a few inches of down trimming such as can be purchased for a few pence in any haberdashery shop or department. One end of this is tied to a length of black carpet twine; the twine is then run around the set across nails fixed at strategic points. On the cue a steady pull from the other end of the twine (this can be done by **Lemuel** UL if you are short of staff) will cause the "denizen" to leap out of **Claud**'s hands. If you have no house tabs, obviously the twine must be set in position before the show starts; the whiffenpoof itself can be put in place (behind the piano) during the preceding interval. When **Claud** puts down his rucksack with his back to the audience he mimes taking the "denizen" out of it—in fact he is picking up the creature; he then turns so that the twine is upstage of him and clear to be pulled. The twine must be above head height, naturally, or the Cast will keep walking into it. As the whiffenpoof moves the Swanee whistle accompanies its movements and the lime, with the iris closed right down, also follows it. This is a very simple but extremely effective sight gag which needs very little preparation and is surprisingly easy to work, provided you have suitable places to place the nails.

The trams also depend on black carpet-twine for their locomotion. The sizes of the trams depend on the size of the hall you intend to play in; their relative proportions should be three to one. Each runs along the twine which is passed through holes in each end of the roof and secured in the wings on each side. Another piece of twine is attached to the front of the tram (simply push it through a small hole and tie a matchstick on the back to stop it slipping out) and run across the stage and tied off. On cue, the small tram, which has been set off L, is pulled across (by **Nellie**, if you are short of hands); on the next cue the larger tram, which has been set off R, is pulled across (by **Lemuel** or **Sir Putrid**). As the trams appear the stage Lights should go off and the lime iris come down to a pin-spot; the lime should also have a flicker-wheel attachment. There are many ways of fixing this up, the simplest being a circular piece of cardboard with holes cut in it; this is held in front of the lime by a centre-spindle and spun by hand (or a strobe may be used instead).

THE MASTER AND THE MAID

On stage: Table DL (which can be set by the **Chairman**). *On it:* **Wife's** hat and bag or parasol

Off stage: (L) Top hat **(Wife)**
Black overcoat **(Maid)**
Feather duster **(Maid)**
(R) Handkerchief with twine **(Husband)**

LIGHTING PLOT

THE MOLECATCHER

General lighting throughout

WHO WILL MAN THE LIFEBOAT?

A beach during a storm

Cue 1 As CURTAIN rises (Page 11)
Flashes of lightning. Lights lower

Cue 2 Steamer appears behind groundrow (Page 11)
Follow spot covers. As steamer sinks follow spot iris closes

Cue 3 1st Soprano enters (Page 12)
Focus DR

Cue 4 End of first chorus: (Page 12)
"... All its dangers braving,
Precious souls to save"
Focus on lifeboat entering LC

Cue 5 End of second verse: (Page 13)
"... See their hands uplifted,
Hear their bitter cry—"
Follow spot picks up Mariner above groundrow. As Mariner sinks close up iris to Black-out

Cue 6 End of second chorus: (Page 14)
"... All its dangers braving—"
Follow spot picks up Mariner. Again Black-out as he sinks. (N.B. During next chorus Mariner twice rises and sinks and should each time be covered by the follow spot)

Cue 7 End of third chorus:
"... All its dangers braving,
Precious souls to save." (Page 14)
Lifeboatmen move US. *Kill the Lights* LC. *Also follow spot picks up Mariner as he appears. Bring up the level* UC *and stop lightning flashes*

Cue 8 End of fourth chorus:
"... All its dangers braving,
Precious souls to save; singing—" (Page 15)
Kill Lighting DR. *Follow spot swings across to pick up Britannia entering on boat-truck* LC. *Also bring in special on Coat of Arms flying in above Britannia*

Cue 9 As Coat of Arms flies out and Britannia exits (Page 15)
Kill special and follow spot

THE TRAM-TRACK TRAGEDY

Cue 1 **Chairman:** "... little Nellie's Bloomers!" (Page 20)
Flash three times. (*Lime picks up Belle.*) *Check down*

Cue 2 **Belle:** "... my dear sister comes!" (Page 20)
Up to full. (*Lime picks up Nellie*)

Cue 3 **Nellie:** "... as you will shortly discover." Entry of **Sir Putrid** UR (Page 23)
Check down. Green lime on him for a few seconds only

Cue 4 **Sir Putrid:** "... may your noses all drop off!" **Sir Putrid** exits (Page 25)
Check up. (*Lime picks up Claud*)

Cue 5 **Claud:** "... I might give you the Willies!" **Claud** exits (Page 28)
Check down. (*Lime picks up Sir Putrid entering* UL)

Cue 6 **Sir Putrid:** "... and never called me Daddy!" **Sir Putrid** exits (Page 29)
Check up. (*Lime picks up Belle entering* UR)

Cue 7 **Belle:** "... wend my fearful way to Paddington Green!" **Belle** exits (Page 30)
Lime out

Cue 8 **Chairman** changes sign over and then sits down (Page 30)
Check down. Alarm rings. (*Lime picks up Sir Putrid entering* UL)

Cue 9 **Belle**: ". . . Hurry! Hurry!" Tram appears from L to R (Page 32)
Stage to Black-out. (*Flicker-light with iris closed right down follows the tram across.*) *As soon as the tram has passed from sight check down to previous state and flicker stops*

Cue 10 **Belle**: "Quick—it's getting closer!" (Page 32)
Again stage to Black-out. (*Flicker-light follows larger tram from* R *to* L.) *Again, as soon as tram has passed from sight flicker stops and lights up to nearly full*

Cue 11 Final "Hurrah!" at the end of the closing number:
Check to full, then Black-out as Cast all bow. Count 4 then full up (Page 36)

THE MASTER AND THE MAID

The follow spot with the flicker attachment should be open white—no filters; the shutters should be adjusted to give a rectangular area of light

Cue 1 **Chairman**: "The Master And The Maid!" (2nd time) (Page 37)
Black-out for 3 seconds then flicker-lime to cover acting area only

Cue 2 **Husband** and **Lover** wink, then exit (Page 39)
Black-out for 3 seconds then bring up special on Chairman

Cue 3 **Chairman**: ". . . very well, monsieur. Reversez-vous!" (Page 39)
Black-out for 3 seconds, then flicker-lime on acting area

Cue 4 **Wife** backs off L carrying topper, then **Husband** backs off L straightening his tie (Page 42)
Black-out for 3 seconds then bring up special on Chairman

Cue 5 **Chairman**: ". . . Vite, monsieur . . . silver plate . . . chop-chop." (Page 42)
Black-out for 3 seconds then flicker-lime to cover acting area, this time running very fast

Cue 6 As action slows down prior to fight: (Page 42)
Slow down flicker (if practicable) to stop when Cast freeze

Cue 7 As action speeds up again: (Page 42)
Speed up flicker to fast speed

Cue 8 **Husband** and **Lover** wink, then exit (Page 42)
Black-out for 3 seconds then bring up special on Chairman and the lime—without flicker—on the acting area for calls
N.B. If the "endless loop" gag is worked for the calls, keep the flicker going

EFFECTS PLOT

THE MOLECATCHER

Nil

WHO WILL MAN THE LIFEBOAT?

Cue 1 As CURTAIN rises (Page 11)
Sound of thunder. Steamer appears behind groundrow (L *or* R), *moves to centre, turns vertical and sinks*

Cue 2 End of first chorus: (Page 12)
". . . All its dangers braving,
Precious souls to save."
Boat-truck comes on two-thirds of its length only

Cue 3 "Britons never never never shall be slaves!" (Page 15)
Boat-truck comes to C *as Coat of Arms flies in. The boat-truck halts for a second and then, on the final musical phrase, continues* R *at rapidly increasing speed. It disappears into the wings and there is a tremendous crash*

THE TRAM-TRACK TRAGEDY

Cue 1 **Claud**: ". . . it only wakes up at night." (Page 26)
Whiffenpoof runs across stage to the sound of a swanee whistle

Cue 2 Start of Scene 2 (Page 30)
An alarm clock sounds for six seconds

Cue 3 **Belle**: "Hurry! Hurry!" (Page 32)
The small tram is pulled across from L *to* R

Cue 4 **Belle**: "Quick—it's getting closer!" (Page 32)
The large tram is pulled across from R *to* L *and a chair or stool is set by the* UL *entrance*

THE MASTER AND THE MAID

Cue 1 **Chairman:** ". . . The Master And The Maid!" (2nd time) (Page 37)
Sound of hand-cranked projector—a bicycle stood upside down on its handlebars and saddle and the pedals being cranked by hand

Cue 2 Husband and Lover wink then exit (Page 39)
Whirring stops

Cue 3 **Chairman:** "Very well, monsieur. Reversez-vous!" (Page 39)
Whirring sound recommences

Cue 4 **Maid** raises L hand in gesture of surprise (Page 40)
Feather duster drops into her hand

Cue 5 **Wife** backs off L carrying topper, and **Husband** backs off L straightening his tie (Page 42)
Whirring stops

Cue 6 **Chairman:** "Vite, monsieur . . . silver plate . . . chop-chop." (Page 42)
Whirring sound recommences much faster

Cue 7 As action slows down prior to fight: (Page 42)
Whirring slows down to stop when Cast freeze

Cue 8 As action speeds up again: (Page 42)
Whirring recommences to very fast speed

Cue 9 **Husband** and **Lover** wink then exit (Page 42)
Whirring stops
N.B. If "endless loop" gag is worked for the calls keep the whirr going

COSTUMES

THE MOLECATCHER

As available. See Notes to the Producer (page x).

WHO WILL MAN THE LIFEBOAT?

The Three Ladies: Summer day-dresses of the 1900 period; with hats, boots, tights, gloves, and R.N.L.I. sashes. The sashes should match the ladies' ensembles, which should be of contrasting (but not clashing) colours.

The **Contralto** will also require: A Britannia robe which can be easily slipped over her day-dress. She will also require a Britannia helmet; the shield and spear can be ready-fixed to the side of the lifeboat.

Mariner: A ragged open-neck shirt, and ragged trousers held up by a piece of string. No shoes or socks.

Lifeboatmen: Sou'westers, oilskins, seaboots or wellingtons. No gloves. If they have a quick change to follow, ordinary period boots may be worn; also, if the oilskins are long enough, the breeches need not be worn to allow the next costume to be under-dressed.

THE TRAM-TRACK TRAGEDY

Belle: A bright frilly blouse and a full-length skirt; not too dressy. She can wear a boa, if available, and should have a boater or leghorn hat trimmed to match the ensemble. Button boots and gloves. Two petticoats under the skirt for fullness.

Nellie: A simple gingham three-quarter-length dress, with a matching bow in the hair; white tights and button boots, a shawl of indeterminate age and colour. She looks rather innocent and childlike.

Lemuel: Corduroy trousers, boots, a fancy blouse-type shirt worn open to the waist showing a Romany-type medallion around his neck. A red kerchief is knotted around his head and a matching sash is around his waist.

Messenger boy: a pillbox over the kerchief. Or an Australian bush-hat.

Driver: a large overcoat, preferably black, and a peaked cap again worn over his kerchief.

Hawkshaw: A deer-stalker hat.

Sir Putrid: A tail or morning suit, with a top hat and a grey waistcoat. He also wears a clerical collar and black stock beneath a false front. This front (to resemble a shirt and cravat) should be made in one piece and split at the back of the neck and given a velcro fastening so that it can be pulled off in one movement. A chain and elaborate fob are worn across the waistcoat.

Conductor: Black cloak and peaked cap.

Claud: Large boots, khaki socks, baggy khaki shorts and a bush-jacket, solar topee and khaki shirt. The shirt is worn buttoned-up but tie-less. He has an identical chain and fob to Sir Putrid's across his chest from breast pocket to breast pocket.

THE MASTER AND THE MAID

N.B. All costumes should be black, white and grey. No colours at all.

Husband: Morning suit, grey waistcoat (or evening tails with a grey waistcoat); white shirt, high starched collar, cravat. Black, highly polished shoes. Gloves. A top hat and a black overcoat. The kind of costume still worn by men in this country at formal weddings would be exactly right.

Wife: A black and white or grey and white ensemble—a white blouse and a black skirt would be the simplest, except that she should contrast with the maid both in appearance and in social class. She has a matching hat and gloves; also a parasol *or* a handbag.

Maid: Long black dress; white apron; white cap.

Lover: White trousers, blazer (striped if possible as long as there are no noticeable colours), a white shirt, low rounded collar and striped (black and white) tie. On his head is a boater with a black or striped band.

If the French Projectionist appears he can be in full evening dress with a star, a sash and medals of various orders. Or he can be slovenly in a blue smock and a beret.

MAKE-UP

THE MOLECATCHER

Make-ups should for all three be basically Leichner 4, plus further variations as discussed in Notes to the Producer (page ix). Keep the eye-shadow light—the three yokels should not look too grotesque.

WHO WILL MAN THE LIFEBOAT?

All players should wear their usual straight make-ups. No heavy characterisations are required in this highly stylised piece.

THE TRAM-TRACK TRAGEDY

Belle: Very glamorous—false eye-lashes, beauty-spot, rouge, etc., etc.

Nellie: Rather pallid, except for the eyes which should be well defined.

Lemuel: Straight, inclining to ruddiness. He wears an ear-ring throughout—preferably a brass curtain-ring on a piece of elastic for easy removal.

Claud: Despite being a big-game hunter he is very pale and wears steel-rimmed spectacles. He could also have a wispy toothbrush moustache—this is more easily painted on than stuck on.

Sir Putrid: Beetle-browed, dark visaged, blue eye-shadow and with a thick black line under the eyes. He also wears a large black moustache which is secured with toupee tape for easy removal and subsequent replacement by Lemuel. As with the other characters his make-up should be strongly characteristic without being overdone—he shouldn't look like a circus clown.

THE MASTER AND THE MAID

All the make-ups for this sketch should be the same: chalk-white faces and heavily accented black eyes and eyebrows. The ladies should have black lipstick; one of the men (but not both) should have a moustache —if the Husband his should be full—he could in fact be bearded—but if the Lover the tache should be small and debonair.

The white can end at the jaw-line; neck, ears and hands can remain unmade-up.

If the French Projectionist appears he should have an Imperial beard, pointed moustaches, hair en brosse and a pince-nez.

PIANO.
1.
THE MOLECATCHER.
INTRO
AFTER NOSE BLOW FROM "C"
M-M-M-MAA......
VERSE
MODERATO
IN AMB-LE SIDE VILL-AGE, AT THE SIGN OF THE PLOUGH, THERE
LIVES A MOLE- CAT-CHER AND I'LL TELL YOU NOW; SIN-GING
CHORUS
Poco
FOL-DE-RUM DAY; FOL-DE-RUM DAY FOL-DE-RUM DIDDLE-DUM
DID-DLE-DUM-DAY.

2.
PIANO TACET THROUGH ROUTINE. PICK UP MELODY
AS THREE PERFORMERS EXIT: N.B. THEY MAY HAVE DROPPED IN PITCH.
F
C7
F
F#
C#7
F#
G
D7
G
Ab
Eb7
Ab

3.
WHO WILL MAN THE LIFEBOAT
STORM
ff
Col 8va
2ND TIME TO CODA
AS BOAT APPEARS
REPEAT FROM 9/8
TILL BOAT STARTS
TO SINK
THEN DA CAPO
CODA
V.S.

4. 1st VERSE
1st. SOPRANO
WHO WILL MAN THE LIFE- BOAT ? WHO THE STORM WILL BRAVE .....
MA - NY SOULS ARE DRIF- TING, HELP-LESS ON THE WAVE .....
SEE THEIR HANDS UP- LIFT- ED, HEAR THEIR BIT- TER CRY ......
2ND SOPRANO + ALTO
f SAVE US ERE WE PER - ISH SAVE US ERE WE DIE ! !! ....

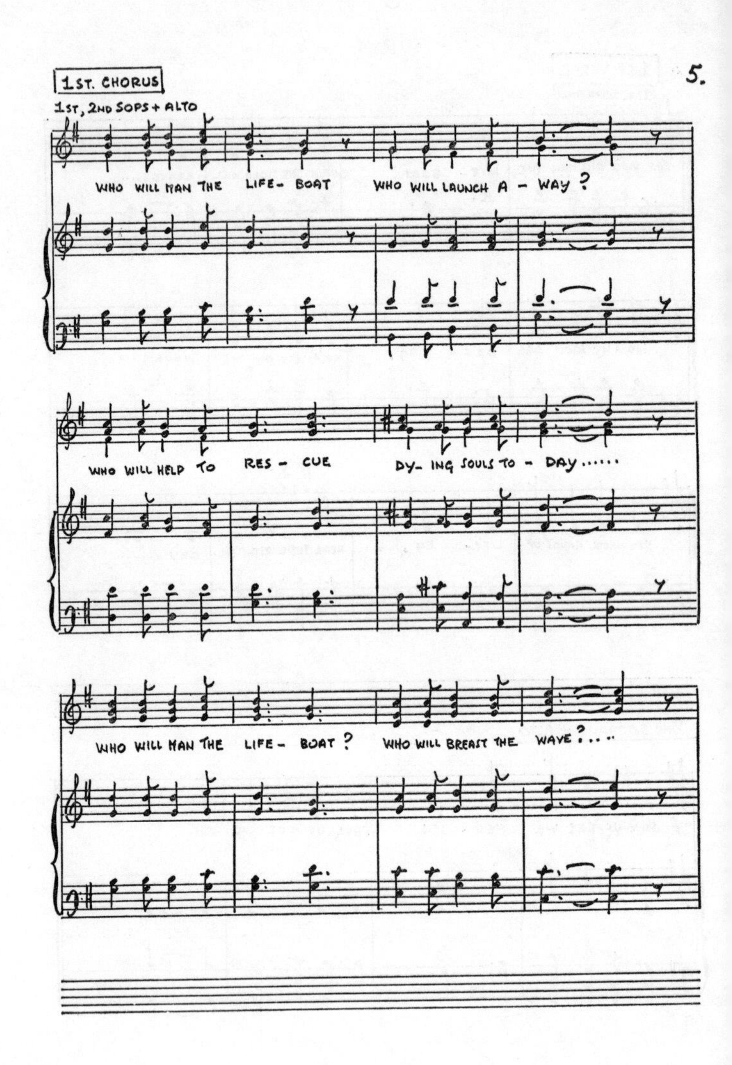
1ST. CHORUS
5.
1ST, 2ND SOPS + ALTO
WHO WILL MAN THE LIFE- BOAT WHO WILL LAUNCH A - WAY ?
WHO WILL HELP TO RES - CUE DY- ING SOULS TO - DAY......
WHO WILL MAN THE LIFE- BOAT ? WHO WILL BREAST THE WAVE ? ...

6.

ALL IT'S DAN-GERS BRA- VING
PRECI-OUS SOULS TO SAVE .....
2ND VERSE [ENTRANCE OF LIFEBOAT]
1, 2, SOPS. + ALTO
WHO WILL MAN THE LIFE- BOAT? WHO THE STORM WILL BRAVE?.. MA-NY SOULS ARE DRIFT-ING.
HELP-LESS ON THE WAVE
SEE THEIR HANDS UP- LIFT-ED, HEAR THEIR BIT-TER

7.

MARINER
CRY.....
SAVE US ERE WE PE-RISH,
SAVE US ERE WE DIE....

2ND CHORUS
1+2 SOPS + ALTO.
SOPS
ALTO
HA — LE - LU - JAH!
THEY WILL HELP TO RES - CUE
LIFEBOATMEN
WE WILL MAN THE LIFE - BOAT WE WILL LAUNCH A - WAY.....

8.
SOPS 1+2
ALTO.
DY- ING SOULS TO - DAY ....
HA — LE —
LIFE-BOATMEN
WE WILL ! WE WILL MAN THE LIFE - BOAT, WE WILL BREAST THE
PIANO
- LU - JAH !
ALL ITS DAN-GERS BRA - VING.
MARINER
WAVE ......
ALL ITS DAN-GERS BRA - VING.
PRE - CIOUS SOULS TO SAVE .....
3RD. CHORUS [PIANO TACET.]
SOP.
ALTO
WHO WILL MAN THE LIFE - BOAT ?
WHO WILL LAUNCH A- WAY ?....
WHO WILL HELP TO
TEN.
BASS

CHOIR
RES- CUE DY- ING SOULS TO- DAY?...
WHO WILL MAN THE LIFE- BOAT.
CHOIR
WHO WILL BREAST THE WAVE?...
ALL ITS DAN- GERS BRA - VING
PRE- CIOUS SOULS TO
4RTH CHORUS
AH
SOPS ALTO
WHO WILL MAN THE LIFE- BOAT? WHO WILL LAUNCH A- WAY.....
TEN BASS
MENO MOSSO
ff
PIANO

10.
AH
AH
CHOIR.
WHO WILL HELP TO RES- CUE. DY- ING SOULS TO DAY! ... (ALTO EXITS) WHO WILL MAN THE LIFE-BOAT ?
AH
AH
WHO WILL BREAST THE WAVE ?..
ALL ITS DANGERS BRA- VING
PRECI-OUS SOULS TO

SAVE......
GIRLS EXIT SINGING
RULE BRI- TANNIA! BRI- TAN-NIA RULES THE WAVES
f
UNIS
BRI- TONS NE-VER NEVER NE-VER SHALL BE SLAVES YES ITS
(EXIT)
1.
BRITTANIA
2.
SHALL..... BE...... SLAVES......
(CRASH)

12.
THE TRAM-TRACK TRAGEDY
TRAM MUSIC
1ST. CUE: "HURRY! HURRY!
2ND CUE: " QUICK ITS GETTING CLOSER "
MODERATO
mf
ff
FADE AS TRAM DISAPPEARS ......

CUE: "SAVED"
CUE: "SIR PUTRID CANKER!"
CUE: "LONG LOST TWIN BROTHER"
CUE: "THE RIGHTFUL BARONET"
CUE: "TWAS ALL A CLERICAL ERROR"
FINALE.
CANKER
OMNES
FOR I AM A CLER-GY - MAN
(SPOKEN) "OF COURSE." FOR
TEMPO
HE HIM-SELF HAS SAID IT, AND ITS GREAT-LY TO HIS CRE-DIT, THAT HE

14.
CANKER
CLAUD
IS AN ANG-LI- CAN....! YES, A HIGH CHURCH ANG-LI - CAN! NOT A
mp
BELLE —. NELLIE —. BOTH LEMUEL
FOLLOW-ER OF JOHN-NY KNOX, NOR GREEK, NOR RUSS-IAN ORTHO-DOX NOR E-
OMNES
- PIS-CO- PA - LI - AN!... NOR E - PIS- CO - PA - LI - AN!... NO, IN
f

15.

SPITE OF ALL TEMP- TA- TIONS, TO BE- LONG TO STRANGE PER-SUA-SIONS, HE RE-
- MAINS AN ANG-LI- CAN HE RE- MAINS... AN AN GLI
RIT...
- CAN. HURRAH! HURRAH! HURRAH! HUR - R AH
THE FOOLS! THE FOOLS! THE FOOLS! THE FOOLS!
TABS FROM
8